Nora the Naturalist's Animals

Pets in the Home

A⁺
Smart Apple Media

Published by Smart Apple Media, an imprint of Black Rabbit Books
P.O. Box 3263, Mankato, Minnesota 56002
www.blackrabbitbooks.com

Produced by David West ☂ Children's Books
7 Princeton Court, 55 Felsham Road, London SW15 1AZ

Designed and illustrated by David West

Copyright © 2013 David West Children's Books

Cataloging-in-Publication data is available from the Library of Congress.
ISBN 978-1-62588-005-5 (library binding)
ISBN 978-1-62588-052-9 (paperback)

Printed in China
CPSIA compliance information: DWCB13CP
010313

9 8 7 6 5 4 3 2 1

Nora the Naturalist says:
I will tell you something
more about the animal.

Learn what this
animal eats.

Where in the
world is the
animal found?

Its size is revealed!

What animal group
is it – mammal, bird,
reptile, amphibian,
insect, or something
else?

Interesting facts.

Contents

Beagle

Dogs

Dogs were probably the first animal to be domesticated. They are kept as a working, hunting, and pet animal in most countries.

Bull Terrier

Dogs are meat eaters.

Dogs are found in homes throughout the world.

Dogs are members of the mammal family.

Dogs vary in size enormously, from a 6-inch (150 mm) Chihuahua to the 2.5 feet (0.76 m) shoulder height of the Irish Wolfhound.

Dogs are one of the few animals to have lived in Antarctica. Now, though, all dogs are banned from living there.

5

Cats eat meat.

 House cats are found in homes throughout the world.

 House cats are generally a uniform size at 10–14 inches (25.4–35.6 cm) at the shoulder.

 Cats are members of the mammal family.

 Cats were worshiped by the ancient Egyptians.

Cats

Cats are the most popular pets in the world. People value them for their friendship, and their ability to hunt rats and mice.

Tortoiseshell and white cat

Siamese cat

7

Rabbits

Domestic rabbits are usually kept as pets in a back yard hutch. They can also be kept indoors if they are house trained. These are often called house rabbits. Many house rabbits can live with the family dog or cat.

New Zealand white

Nora the Naturalist says: House rabbits can live as long as 8–12 years.

Rabbits are plant eaters.

House rabbits are found in homes throughout the world.

Rabbits can grow up to 20 inches (50 cm) in length and weigh more than 10 pounds (4.5 kg).

Rabbits are members of the mammal family.

Rabbits eat their own droppings to get the full amount of nourishment from the plants they eat.

Cashmere Lop

9

Guinea Pigs

This little **rodent** has enjoyed being a household pet in Europe since the 16th century, when traders brought it back from South America.

Two-colored guinea pig

Nora the Naturalist says:
The common guinea pig was first domesticated by Andean tribes for food.

Single-colored guinea pig

Grass is the guinea pig's natural food.

Originally from South America, these pets can now be found all over the world. They can no longer be found in the wild.

They are rodents that belong to the mammal family.

Guinea pigs weigh around 1.5–2.5 pounds (700–1200 g), and measure between 8–10 inches (20–25 cm) in length.

Scientists have used guinea pigs to carry out tests since the 17th century. This has led to the term, "guinea pig," being used for human test subjects.

Hamsters

Hamsters are popular as pets due to their small size and their cute appearance. They are similar looking to a mouse but they are stockier, and don't have a long tail.

Nora the Naturalist says: Hamsters have a pouch on each side of their mouths that extends to their shoulders. They stuff them full of food to be eaten back at their nest.

Golden hamster

Hamsters' diets include dried food, berries, nuts, fresh fruits, and vegetables. In the wild they will also eat insects.

 Hamsters are originally from Syria and Turkey. Today they can be found as pets in many countries around the world.

 The European hamster grows up to 5 inches (13 cm) long.

 Hamsters are rodents that belong to the mammal family.

 Hamsters have poor eyesight. To make up for this, their senses of smell and hearing are very good.

Colored hamster

13

House mice primarily feed on plant matter, but will eat most things they find.

The house mouse is originally from Asia but has spread with humans throughout the world.

Small pet mice are approximately 6–7 inches (15–17.5 cm) long, from the nose to the tip of their tail.

Mice are small mammals that belong to the rodent family.

House mice are mainly active at night.

House mice

14

Mice

Mice may appear in our homes as scavenging pests. Or they may be welcome residents, along with other small pet rodents, such as rats, hamsters, and gerbils.

Nora the Naturalist says:
Although a wild animal, the house mouse mainly lives with humans, causing damage to crops and stored food. The domesticated pet variety is known as a fancy mouse.

Budgerigars eat seeds.

Budgerigars are native to Australia but can be found in pet shops around the world.

Budgerigars are parrots and members of the bird family.

Wild budgerigars average 7 inches (18 cm) in length and weigh 1.1–1.4 ounces (30–40 g)

Budgies have been bred in captivity with coloring of blues, whites, yellows, and grays.

Nora the Naturalist says:
Budgerigars, also known as budgies, are one of the top five talking parrot species.

Yellow budgerigar

Small Birds

Small birds have long been kept as pets in many homes. They include canaries and many types of parrot. The most well known are budgerigars. These small, seed-eating parrots are originally from Australia.

Blue budgerigar

17

Macaws

These are large, brightly-colored parrots. Their ability to talk, and to bond closely to humans makes them popular pets.

Blue and yellow macaw

Scarlet macaw

Nora the Naturalist says:
There are 19 different species of macaw. Most of them live in rainforests, although some like open woodland.

18

Green macaw

Macaws eat all sorts of food, from seeds, nuts, and fruit to the occasional pieces of meat or fish.

Originally from South and central America, these birds can now be found in homes all over the world.

Macaws are parrots and members of the bird family.

These birds can reach 34 inches (86 cm) long and weigh 1.9 to 3.3 pounds (900 to 1500 g).

Macaws, like toucans, woodpeckers, and other parrots, have their first and fourth toes pointing backwards.

19

Goldfish

These popular household pets can be kept in ponds, or in aquariums in the house. The fancy telescope eye, or demekin, is named after its protruding eyes. It is also known as globe eye, or the dragon eye goldfish.

Pet goldfish are fed fish food.

Goldfish are found in pet stores, and aquarium specialty stores around the world.

They may grow to around 6–8 inches (15–20 cm) long, and occasionally even longer.

Goldfish are a relatively small member of the carp family.

Goldfish are gold colored in response to light. If left in the dark they change color to gray.

Nora the Naturalist says: First domesticated in China more than a thousand years ago, several breeds have been developed. They vary greatly in size, body shape, fin configuration, and color.

Globe eye goldfish

Tropical Fish

Tropical fish are popular as aquarium fish. Their bright colors and unusual shapes are real eye catchers. Tropical fish that live in the sea are kept in salt water aquariums.

Butterfly fish

Nora the Naturalist says:
Some butterfly fish have a marking that looks like an eye near their tail. This fools hungry fish into thinking they will move in a different direction.

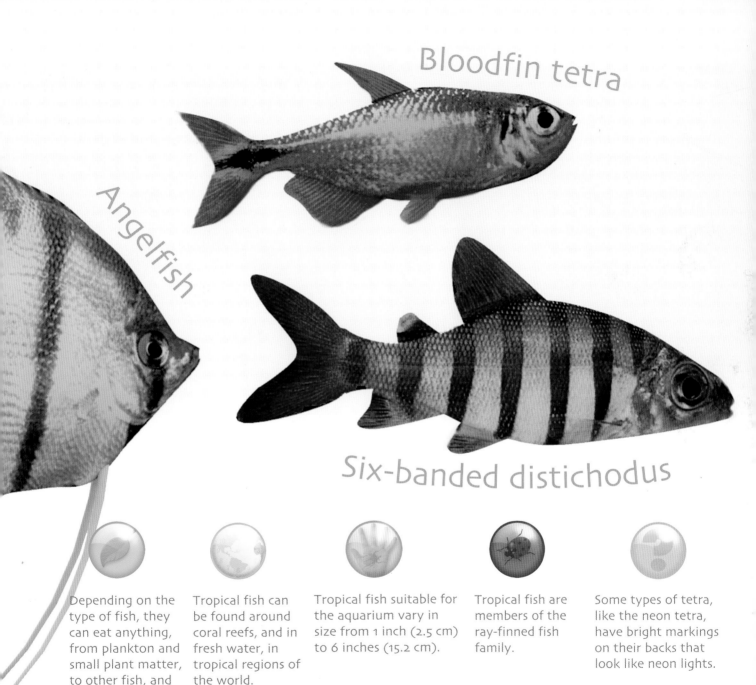

Bloodfin tetra

Angelfish

Six-banded distichodus

Depending on the type of fish, they can eat anything, from plankton and small plant matter, to other fish, and even coral.

Tropical fish can be found around coral reefs, and in fresh water, in tropical regions of the world.

Tropical fish suitable for the aquarium vary in size from 1 inch (2.5 cm) to 6 inches (15.2 cm).

Tropical fish are members of the ray-finned fish family.

Some types of tetra, like the neon tetra, have bright markings on their backs that look like neon lights.

23

Glossary

domestication
The changing of a species of animal over time, so that it becomes useful to humans, as a work or farm animal, or as a pet.

rodent
An order of mammals that includes mice, rats, squirrels, porcupines, beavers, guinea pigs, and hamsters. They have a single pair of continuously growing front teeth which are kept short by gnawing.

Index